5th Jan. 1992

.To Hilda,
   With lots & lots of love,
      from Roberta.

NEW ZEALAND
GIFT *of the* SEA

NEW ZEALAND
GIFT *of the* SEA

BRIAN BRAKE
MAURICE SHADBOLT

Hodder & Stoughton
AUCKLAND LONDON SYDNEY TORONTO

Photographs: Brian Brake
Text and commentaries: Maurice Shadbolt
Photo editors: Raymond W.M. Lau, Maurice Shadbolt
    and Donna Hoyle
Designer: Donna Hoyle

Typeset by Typocrafters Ltd, Auckland
Printed and bound by
Everbest Printing Co. Ltd, Hong Kong,
for Hodder & Stoughton Ltd,
44–46 View Road, Glenfield,
Auckland, New Zealand.

Contents

*T*welve years ago, soon after his return to his native New Zealand as one of the world's most celebrated photographers, Brian Brake and I began planning a large book on New Zealand, one which would use image and word to tell the land's story from its primal beginnings — a volume far more substantial than our youthful collaboration of the 1960s, *New Zealand: Gift of the Sea*, but with the same theme. The new version of *Gift of the Sea*, we hoped, would range wider and deeper; it would also be visually richer.

For much of a decade Brian quietly gathered material for such a book. He was still working on it on 4 August 1988 — perhaps a month short of satisfying himself that he had sufficient material to hand — when he died suddenly in his Titirangi, Auckland home.

It has been my often poignant task to complete our collaboration alone, and nurse the book into final form; I could never have done so without the help of Brian's dedicated and sensitive associate, Lau Wai Man. Brian, as it turned out, left us a feast of images to tell the story of New Zealand and its people, in the way we most wished to tell it. My hope now is that this book proves a durable memorial to a much-loved friend, collaborator and neighbour, that impish and modest magician with a camera, named Brian Brake.

Maurice Shadbolt
Titirangi
December 1989

CREATION'S FIVE MILLION YEARS

There was light on the waters, and land in the light.

Phantom crumbs of a lost continent
left to the world's waters.

Fire fought water.

Molten mountains roared
from the planet's core.

As ice ebbed, insurgent sea drowned valleys and left islands swarming.

Rushing far into the land, sea fashioned fiord and long harbour.

Life's tide rose too.

Everywhere leaf and flower, long in retreat, coloured the land again.

In this lonely
corridor of creation,
nature was both
playful and powerful.

Lizards lost to the world lived here, yet hardly
a mammal, and never the mammal called man.

Creatures of sea, creatures of shore.

Creatures of forest, creatures of river.

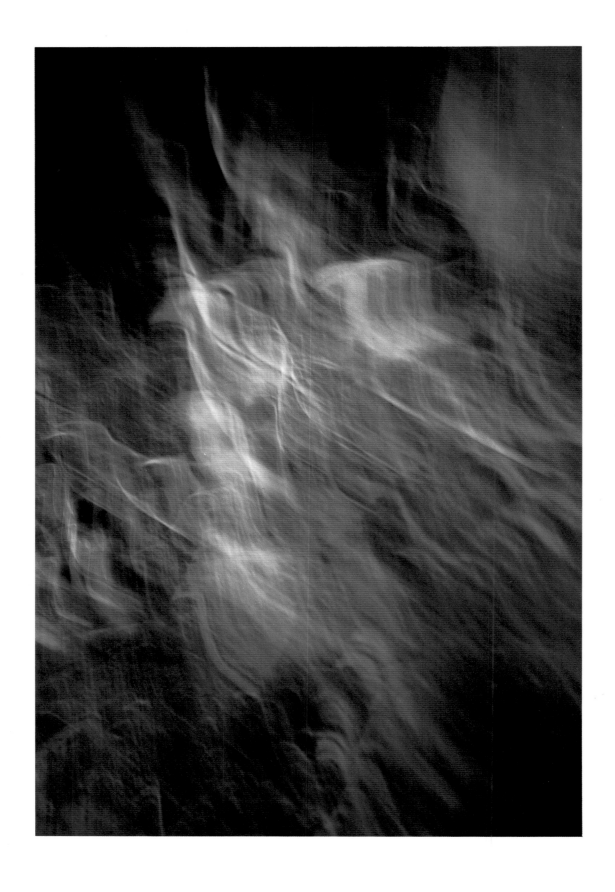

Otherwise it was a land empty of lovers.

Elsewhere in the world man had left African desert to harvest rather than hunt. Villages of thatch had become cities of stone. Civilisations had risen and fallen, with art and religion their residue. Homer had long sung the Iliad and Odyssey. Confucius and Christ, Mohammed and Buddha had already had their earthly say. Yet there was still no human print here, no nomad campfire, no sound save that of wind, water and bird.

A mere five million years in the making, in geologic time New Zealand is a fledgling, hardly a heartbeat older than the human race itself, an impish afterthought on the part of the planet. It was to be the last frontier for the human species.

Risen upright in Africa three million or more years ago, our furthest ancestors toiled across tall mountain ranges and rafted across river and sea to hunt, gather, and seed the planet with their own kind: all Africa, Europe, Asia, and before long the Americas fell to the two-legged newcomers. Few natural fastnesses were left unstormed as our species sledded across seas of ice and canoed through perilous archipelagos. Three or four thousand years ago the long march of humankind might have seemed complete. Now more than nomadic, man looked to have won the planet. Animals were herded and husbanded rather than wearily hunted; the fruits of the earth were grown rather than gathered. Thatched villages announced the arrival of tribes; stone towns and cities the beginnings of civilisations. Metals were won from the rocks of the earth, and fashioned into weapon and tool. The written word had arrived; and the wheel.

Yet there was still the Pacific. There was one third of the planet unknown and unmastered, with hundreds of habitable islands empty of human sound. The push out of Asia began perhaps 3000 years ago. By 1000 A.D. generations of Polynesians, as they would later be called, had sailed into the sunrise to claim most of those islands for *Homo sapiens* too. Their largest trophy was tall New Zealand, in the far south: it comprised 90 per cent of Polynesia's land area. By contrast with the tiny tropical islands and atolls they left behind, these navigators found New Zealand an uncannily cool world of long surf-beaten beaches, rain forest and great river, shimmering mountain, thundering waterfall and rumbling volcano, a land still smoking with the fires that formed it, still shaking from the convulsions which lofted its peaks 3000 metres or more into the sky. It was the last land of substance Polynesians were to settle, and for that matter the human race. Another 1000 years on, it would become Europe's last frontier too. For these later arrivals New Zealand was as much a mystery as it was for the first Polynesian. Science is still tallying its character, telling us how the land came to be.

What baffled early European explorers and naturalists in New Zealand was the distinctive and diverse character of its evergreen forest, the flamboyant range of birds flighted and flightless, and above all the absence of mammals. Free of mammalian predators, many birds had no use for flight; they safely foraged and nested on forest floor. At first no one could make much of the mysterious absence of mammals. For a time some surmised that these islands had once been linked to continents by land-bridges which had eroded away after the appearance of plant and bird but before the appearance of animals on the planet. But New Zealand rocks weren't kin to continental: they were oceanic. New Zealand's 27 million hectares were a gift of the sea, composed mostly of compacted sub-marine sediment forced from the sea floor.

Yet the land was no virgin birth: it had begun as crumbs of a greater landmass. Once an appendage of a supercontinent named Gondwanaland, until the Tasman Sea began forming more than 60 million years ago, New Zealand — or the great-grandparent of New Zealand — had parted company with continents. At first it was possibly no more than a cluster of steamy islands and misty shoals linking Australia and Antarctica. Elsewhere most such archipelagos perished, bitten down to stumps and reefs by powerful seas. New Zealand, or some of what was to be New Zealand, survived. But wandering and island-hopping species of plant, bird and reptile migrated here from greater Gondwana, including the ancestors of such unique species as the tuatara, now the world's most ancient reptile. Even the celebrated kiwi, without a feather to fly on, managed to shuffle short-sightedly aboard. But with a marine gap growing between New Zealand and Australia, the land went into lofty isolation, aloof from the rest of the world. Dinosaurs had disappeared as they had elsewhere. Birds and flowering plants, on the other hand, flourished; relics from the dawn of life, lizard and frog, still romped and wriggled over forest floor. Apart from tiny bush bats blown in from Australia, New Zealand was long to be denied mammals, and in particular the lethal mammal called man.

Meanwhile creation had a vivid playground. More than 80 per cent of New Zealand's flowering plants are peculiar to the country, likewise all twenty species of conifers, such as the kauri and rimu, though some have kin in South-east Asia, Australia and South America. Palms like the ti (cabbage tree) and nikau tell of the time when the land was tropical: they adapted and survived as the land cooled to temperate. Ferns, more than anything else, give character to the New Zealand forest, from filmy mites to monsters 16 metres tall. The kauri tree, the elephant of the vegetable world, falls just short of being the world's tallest and longest living tree (it ranks second to California's sequoia on both scores), but is by far the bulkiest; it can soar 55 metres, with a girth of 16 metres, all of 2000 years old.

Birds could be as robust. Making themselves native after land-links were lost, or arriving as colonists from far shores, they took on colourful character in oceanic isolation, from tiny to tall. Most spectacularly, there was the house-high moa, gently grazing grassland, as big a bird as the world has known.

The ice ages — beginning two million years ago, and persisting until perhaps 10,000 B.C. with perverse patches of warmth between — put plant and bird to their first great test. Many species expired. In the south most forest vanished as glaciers gripped the land. Some flora and fauna made a tactical retreat to havens in the warmer north. Three of the land's best-known species — the kauri, mangrove, and cliff-hanging pohutukawa — would remain there and never return. But even much of the north, lashed by bitter wind, was no more than miserable shrubland and grassland. On the other hand, in the south, the ebb and flow of glaciation gave sturdy alpine plants a chance to meet, mingle, and hybridise fresh species. The celmisia (the New Zealand mountain daisy), or the Mount Cook lily, are thus more truly native than the silver fern which the nation takes as its emblem. For that matter, the shy, snuffling and nocturnal kiwi — our other national emblem — is not half so astonishing and original a creature as the bold and snook-cocking mountain parrot New Zealanders know as the kea. It grew as the South Island's mountains climbed from the sea, flying higher as less heroic parrots loitered in lowland forest; and took the ice age, as it would the arrival of man, in its stride.

Ice age and aftermath were to sculpt the country we now call New Zealand. The earth's old fires had formed it: undersea cataclysm had given it bulk; the ocean had bitten out its rough silhouette; now great rivers of ice ground it smooth. With the retreat of the glaciers, wind and water began work. Mountains were whittled down by wild storm and waterfall: waterborne debris built plain. The process is still on powerful show in the South Island. The valleys which lead up to the retreating Fox and Franz Josef glaciers are literal laboratories of creation, as awesome as the glaciers themselves, with growth slowly establishing itself at their foot and forest beginning again to form. The visitor is witness to the world in the making. Thus did life's tide rise through the land when the last ice age was gone. Frosty winds no longer withered vegetation to the north; in something less than 500 years forest was again rising high. Even in the cooler south, embattled bastions of forest were liberated and rushed to colour new territory. Birdlife, long on the wane, began to ring loud through the land again.

Even more dramatically, the end of the ice age meant a lift in the sea levels as shrinking glaciers, conspicuously in Antarctica, disgorged the world's locked-up waters. Rising ocean raced deep into the land, drowning valleys, fashioning great fiords, scuttling hills to leave their summits as sea-lapped islands. Above all it separated New Zealand's two major islands by filling the tear-fault now called Cook Strait. Gowned extravagantly in green, the land was a bold-eyed bride with no groom. Earthquake and eruption might lift it or shift it: rivers might change course and mountains inch higher. But essentially New Zealand was in business. The question was, with whom?

MAN'S FIRST THOUSAND YEARS

*Sailing out of Asia into the sunrise,
Polynesian voyagers made the islands of the Pacific their own.
To the south they beached their canoes on the boldest of all.*

Strange mountains soared inland.

Lakes loomed the size of seas.

There was beauty.
There was mystery.

Ice was new,
and smouldering mountains.

It was a land asking legend.

Stories would soon haunt headland, harbour and hill.

The first to make their mark
saw a land warred over by good and evil, gods and demons.

Men warred over it too.
Their fortresses would leave a lasting mark.

It was a warrior culture.
The Maori had no name but that of his tribe.

Tattoo spoke for the warrior.
His was not merely to master the enemy;
his was to challenge all earth and sky.

In life's fevers they found a vivid art.

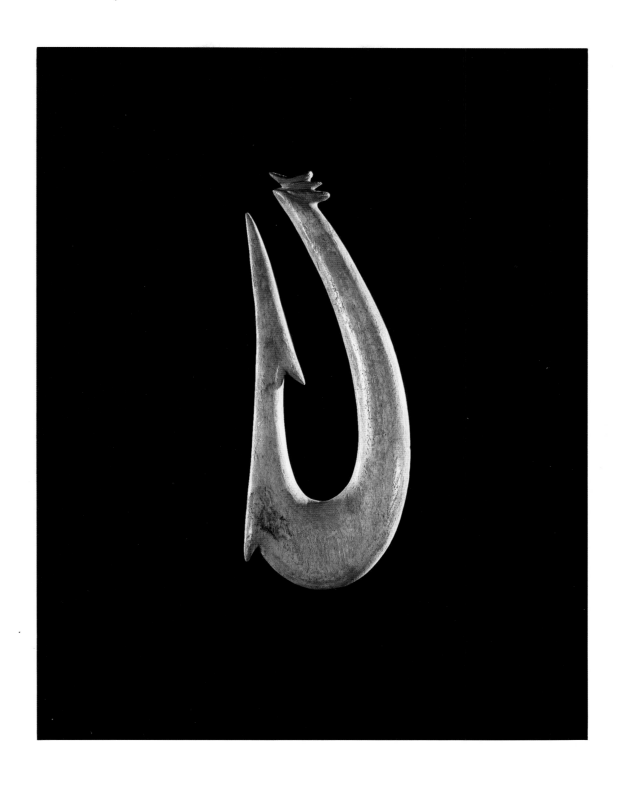

They looked into wood, stone and bone,
and gave it their story.

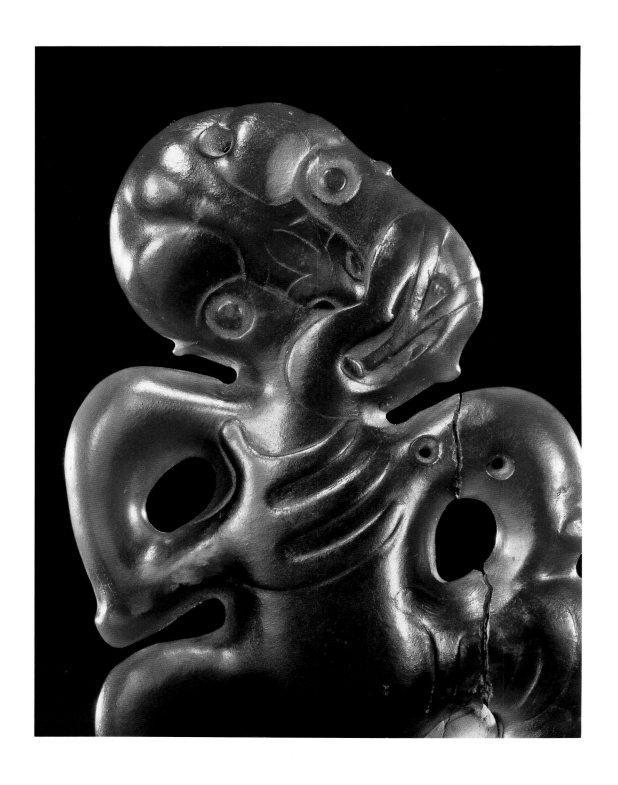

*They worked with what
the new land gave them.*

Their treasures still speak from
the silences of the past.

The tale of a far Queen,
and a crucified Christ,
found a new home here.

There would be new faiths.

New prophets.
New fortresses, new wars.

Much was lost. Much was not.

*Close to the heart of
most Maori is the tribe.
At the heart of the tribe
is the marae.*

An epic past is still cause for pride.

For grief, feast or fellowship, the marae is home.

Yesterday dwells here. Tomorrow too.

Three thousand years ago, perhaps more, a small band of people began moving out from the shore of south China. Persecution, deprivation or population pressure, or all three, may have spurred them to leave terra firma behind. All we need know here is that they made themselves the most formidable mariners the world has seen. The wisdom of one generation of seafarers was to be enriched by the next.

Over centuries they voyaged through the islands of the Malay archipelago, and skirted the northern coast of New Guinea, settling islands here and there as they moved. Finally and dramatically, they let their sails tug them further, into the aweingly empty Pacific. Many must have perished of hunger, thirst and despair as they felt through the ocean for land and life; others found fertile islands and multiplied. As population grew and resources diminished, new voyagers would again chance all on fresh islands beyond the horizon. There would be no tales of failure to terrify them. Tradition would tell only of successful voyages. What their forebears had done, they could too. They gambled on sun, stars, floating leaves, migrant birds, the shape of waves and the colour of the sea.

In a millenium or two this astonishing people had colonised almost every useful scrap of land in the Pacific. The scale of this feat cannot be overstated. Europeans were still paddling about such lake-like seas as the Baltic and Mediterranean, seldom out of sight of land. It wasn't until the fifteenth century A.D. that such island groups as the Azores were found in the mid-Atlantic. Even Columbus's discovery of the Americas in 1492 appears puny. He may have been aimed at India, but how could he miss? Yet many Polynesian islands were lonely coral specks, hundreds of nautical miles from neighbours. Even when clustered they sat faint on the horizon, easily missed in storm or dark. How they were all found is still debated. Some obstinately see chance, drift voyages, lost fishermen. Chance fails to explain the settling of Hawaii, to the far north, or New Zealand, to the remote south, let alone diminutive Easter Island to the distant east.

Such a harvest had to be the prize of a deliberate and deadly lottery. The story of man in New Zealand — the largest land on which Polynesians were to beach their long ocean-going canoes — began on heroic scale: there was a task even more heroic ahead. Finding New Zealand was one thing. Surviving it was another.

Archaeology says that it is 1000 years since the first human being settled here, or yesterday in humankind's calendar. The temperate shore must never have been less than challenging to a tropical people. One thing is plain. When they came, they came as colonisers and not ocean vagrants. They arrived with useful plants and animals, though not with all they might have. They probably tried to bring the domestic pig, and failed; perhaps its flesh had become too tempting on the long voyage out of eastern Polynesia. But they landed the dog and the rat for consumption. New Zealand was out of creation's closet. Mammals, and conspicuously man, were loose on the land.

Even so, man had a long and hard campaign to win a home. Most tropical food crops, the coconut, banana, and breadfruit, refused to take root. It was a battle for the new arrivals to raise even familiar root crops like the kumara, or sweet potato, and taro. Pounded fern root would become a substitute, as well as the not especially nourishing fruits and berries of the New Zealand forest. On the other hand the rivers and seas were rich with fish, shores with seal, and the forest with fat and strange birds. The peacefully leaf-browsing moa, in some 25 species, ranging from one metre tall to three, early began falling back before human advance. At the beginning it may have been the major food source. But the hunt was wasteful, with fire often used to flush the creatures from forest, and the toll terrible. Sometimes no more than a limb of the bird was eaten and the rest left to rot. There was no halt to the killing, nor to the fires which left land naked and destroyed warm micro-climates — especially in the south — where the kumara could grow comfortably. Within two or three centuries the moa was rare: by the time Europeans arrived it was a rumour. It was one of more than a dozen species of bird to disappear forever after the arrival of the Polynesian. The rat and the dog cleared much that humans didn't; the tuatara survived only on wispy islands off the mainland.

The first voyagers made other adaptions. The paper mulberry tree, from which Polynesians made bark cloth, or *tapa*, failed to grow to more than a miserable size. Native flax was called into service and stripped and woven for the warm garments needed for comfort in New Zealand. Housing presented problems too. When winter winds blew, the simple airy dwellings of tropical Polynesia no longer sufficed. Houses were sunk in the earth, with a thick thatch and solid posts of dressed timber. These would become even more elaborate and weatherproof. The new land demanded new crafts.

The land had one bonus. For craftsman and artist there were raw materials beyond the reach of a tropical islander's: a wealth of stone, bone and timber made marvels possible. The giant trees of the forest — totara and kauri — could be felled, hollowed and carved for huge and stable canoes; a balancing outrigger was no longer needed. There was jade (or New Zealand *pounamu*, 'greenstone') for ornament, adornment, weapon and tool. There was obsidian, a volcanic glass with a fine cutting edge, for those who dressed flax for fine cloaks. There was whalebone from the carcasses of ocean giants slain or cast up on its shores.

Yet at the heart of New Zealand's prehistory there is an enigma. Archaeology has established that there were two Polynesian cultures: one early, one late. The early, now called moa-hunter or archaic Maori, seems to have been relatively simple and rather nomadic, a society of wandering hunters and gatherers. They still speak to us across centuries in faded cave paintings and carvings which seem to have been their work. The second culture would eventually prevail: it is now called classic Maori. This society was to be distinguished by a settled mode of existence, typified by large hilltop fortifications or *pa*, dedication to agriculture, and the digging of food storage pits to defy barren seasons. Weapons of close combat, and cannibalism as a consequence of war, were a feature of this society too. This was the teasing and sometimes terrifying stone-age culture seen flourishing when Europeans arrived in the eighteenth century.

The puzzle for archaeologists is whether the second culture derived from the first, or whether it was imposed on the original colonists by a belligerent band of later voyagers. Those opting for evolution see a clue in climate change in the thirteenth and fourteenth centuries. Areas suitable for growing the staple of the Maori diet, the kumara, began shrinking. Land still useful for horticulture had to be defended; fortifications began to proliferate, and fights over fertile soil. But war became more than a means to an end. It served *mana* (status) or *utu* (vengeance) and was an end in itself. There were seasons for fishing, seasons for growing, and seasons for war. One uncelebrated motive for war must have been the acquisition of slaves, those spared by war parties for future and menial function. Archaeology cannot tell us much about their existence, though songs, legends and placenames suggest it sad and short.

On the other hand their captors didn't have it much better. Pre-European New Zealand was no earthly paradise. Human remains tell us that life was as brief and brutal here as it was in other stone-age societies. Those who lived past thirty were aged, feeble and heir to most human afflictions. Violent death was never a distant prospect. Existence must often have been a numbing struggle. Pressure on land grew with population; wars, it would seem, became more ferocious. Those defeated often limped from the warm north to less hospitable land in the south, and even there could be harassed to extinction, as the moa before them.

Maori theology was filled with warring gods and reckless heroes. Even original creation had been a bitter affair. The story begins with the Sky-father (*Rangi*) and the Earth-mother (*Papa*) clinging together in prolonged sexual embrace; their many progeny dwelt suffocatingly in the dark between their parents' bodies. Restless and rebellious, they cruelly conspired to part their parents forever. Tane, the strong young god of the forest, finally pushed Rangi high, and light flooded in upon his fellow offspring. The tears of Rangi thereafter fell as rain upon his wife Papa, while her grief at their separation rose as mist. Life, in the Maori version of events, began in no sunlit Eden, but in a Vale of Tears. The industrious Tane went on to create a daughter from clay and, out of incestuous liaison, the first man.

Among other Maori antecedents was the mighty folk-hero Maui, whose feats are recorded elsewhere in Polynesia. With the jawbone of his grandmother as potent weapon, he snared the sun and brought fire to earth. On a fishing trip with his older brothers he caught — to their dismay — a giant fish with his grandmother's ubiquitous jawbone. It proved to be New Zealand's North Island. In jealous rage his brothers hacked at the sea monster, which explains the North Island's rugged aspect. In some versions of the Maui story the South Island is said to be Maui's canoe, and diminutive Stewart Island his anchorstone. Maui's final task was an attempt to win immortality for mankind. He sought it head-first between the parted thighs of Hine-nui-te-po, the goddess of darkness and death, as she slept. A laughing bird, friend of Maui, gave the game away; she woke, closing her legs, and he strangled in her vagina before he could make total entrance to her body. Earth triumphed over spirit: man thereafter was doomed to die.

Maori art, as expressed in carving and chant, was complex, abstract and allusive, a distillation of tribal experience and a challenge to fate. Wood was not the only material for the carver to work; human flesh, the face of the warrior, served well too. The task of the warrior was not merely to master the enemy but to best the world in open encounter and test the limits of human mortality, much as Maui when he chanced all to win life everlasting.

Numbers grew. New Zealand was settled by perhaps 20,000 people of Polynesian origin in the twelfth century. By the eighteenth there may have been ten times as many. The Maori was by far the most numerous and powerful of Polynesia's scattered peoples. On the other hand — living in an isolated culture with little but legend to tell of its beginnings — Maori had no notion of themselves as members of a race; they certainly never saw themselves as a nation. Their identity was that of their tribe; their life was the tribe, and tribes were many. 'Maori' was merely the word by which they identified themselves when Europe's voyagers first arrived: it means 'normal', which Europeans were visibly not.

This was the stage on to which Captain James Cook stumbled in 1769. New Zealand arrived in history at last. But prehistory had already scripted much of the drama to come. Innocent of the outside world, and with no national sense — still feuding with their own kind rather than with the pale newcomers — the Maori people were poorly placed to survive Europe's tide.

Yet they would; they did. The story of the Maori, since Britain took New Zealand as a colony under the Treaty of Waitangi in 1840, is that of a people winning their way back into the sun from disaster, despair and possible extinction. The nineteenth century would bring the Christian faith; it also brought unfamiliar viruses and the firearm. Disease and musket wars — fought between tribe and tribe — levelled many. Challenges to Queen Victoria's authority, in the middle of the century, would lower more. Loss of land, whether vengefully confiscated, or spirited away by speculators, would diminish those who survived. The fight back began at the turn of the century. It was a battle for the spirit of the race, to be won by pride rather than firepower, to be led by visionaries rather than traditional chiefs. And it is a battle still being fought. Success can be measured by statistics. At the beginning of the twentieth century the Maori race numbered few more than 40,000. Now it numbers ten times as many, with tens of thousands more New Zealanders of mixed blood and proud of their Maori heritage. That heritage, with the Maori language, has never been more celebrated as a nation's treasure than it is today.

Not all seas promise smooth, but the descendants of Polynesia's great mariners have surely seen out the worst of the storm. It is not just a tale of survival; it is one of triumph.

TWO HUNDRED HEADLONG YEARS

Dutch voyagers reported a land lifting high.

Wild sea and wild warrior turned them away.

In another century
British voyagers made landfall.

In warm northern harbours, whalers had a haven.

In cold southern fiords, sealers made camp.

Voyagers braved tidal highways to bargain for timber and flax.

Carpenters for Christ,
the missionaries came to stay.

They left durable dwellings.
Lasting churches.

In the south, cob houses of sheepmen rose in hostile highland.

They pushed their flocks higher still.

Goldseekers gusted into the land's empty places.

They fossicked in dank forest.

They enriched high acres with their relics.

Graves tell of lone and loveless lives.

Fire slew forest.

It bared the body of the land.

God-fearing pioneers came to master new earth, and did.

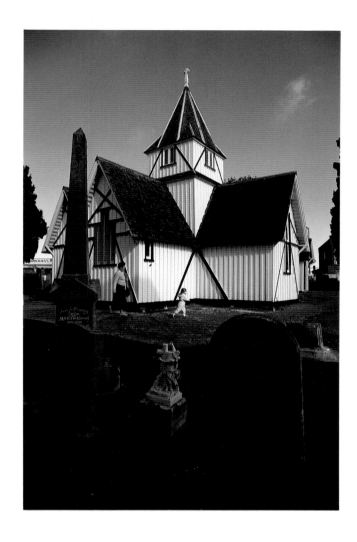

They gave thanks to God
lyrically in wood.

Mightily in stone.

The length of the land, Europe's forms lifted.

Large and small,
their message was plain.

A message scented with the trees and flowers of far lands.

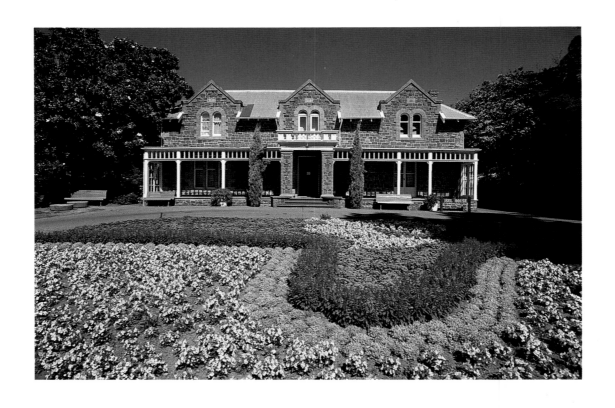

*Migrants of more than one race
now called these islands home.*

The first European navigator to burst into the Pacific was Magellan in 1520. Others followed. Looking for riches, they found no new realms of gold and silver, no opulent continents. There was just island after humble island in a vast ocean, populated by a brown and bold people hitherto unknown to Europe. It was more than another century before a Dutch voyager named Abel Tasman, sailing from the west, and venturing south, found himself, in December 1642, off a stormy shore backed by great mountains. His map of the western shore of this 'land uplifted high' suggested a continent's edge. Imaginative cartographers would soon invent an eastern shore extending almost to South America. In Tasman's one attempt to land he clashed bloodily with Maori, and lost four crewmen. Elsewhere he thought he saw giants. At all events, he fast sailed home again. His mercantile employers were not impressed: he had no report of riches.

Nevertheless the notion of a great South Sea continent haunted Europeans for more than a dozen decades. The problem was establishing its location. For those lost on its waters the Pacific was still as deadly as for the Polynesians who first braved it. The new voyagers on the ocean were reluctant to risk the cool, stormy and scurvy-ridden latitudes in which Tasman's mystery land lay. Maybe there was a continent waiting: there might also be death in dark waters.

Much of the problem was technical. Europeans could measure latitude accurately, but not longitude. This changed with the development of the chronometer in the eighteenth century. The voyager who used it to most dramatic effect was James Cook. He arrived in the Pacific in 1769 on the first of three world-shaking voyages into the unknown south — so far south, once, that Antarctic ice fouled his rigging. He found no continent. But he did trawl one green prize from turbulent waters. That prize was New Zealand, nowhere near a continent, but a land roughly the size of his native Britain. Even on his first voyage Cook saw the potential of this temperate and fertile land for European colonisation. He circumnavigated it, mapping its coast with few mistakes, and learning to make friends with the Maori after a first, confused attempt to land left tribesmen dead. Thereafter, often at great personal risk, the prudent and humanitarian Cook chanced no clashes. New Zealand became his base and haven. His reports to London on New Zealand and its inhabitants left a powerful impression. Not that there was any rush — or even thought — to colonise the country. Even as Cook was voyaging, Britain was bitterly counting the cost of its rebellious American colonies. Colonies were not in favour.

Soon the sails of other adventurers and explorers lit New Zealand's horizons. Britain's convict settlements in Australia, begun in 1788, brought the world still closer. It was only a matter of time before New Zealand was eyed covetously. First ashore was a Sydney-recruited sealing gang, in Fiordland, in 1792. In ten months they harvested 4500 sealskins for the Asian market. In remote Dusky Sound, following a shipwreck in 1795, there was even a castaway community of 200 people for most of two years. They left, but other sealers moved in to establish beachheads for Europe. Encampments, then ramshackle villages, grew on southern shores. Many sealers came to stay, marrying into Maori tribes. The slaughter of New Zealand's teeming seal population paralleled the destruction of the moa centuries before. In the early 1800s the brutal business grew. One American captain sailed for Sydney with 60,000 skins.

A larger creature drew mariners to the northern extreme of the country. Salty hunters from Plymouth and Nantucket rejoiced in the great whale herds spouting off the New Zealand coast. These voyagers made bases in such eastern harbours as the Bay of Islands, where they could render down their hard-won blubber and roister until the next hunt. Soon there were semi-permanent settlements — with butchers, bakers, grog shops and brothels serving nautical appetites — risen here too. In Northland, as in Southland, such settlements were not possible without the active collaboration of Maori tribes; their chiefs turned entrepreneurs, with an eye to profit and power. Muskets to settle old scores ranked high among their requirements. Bought or bartered, these new weapons were soon smoking away rival tribes. Some virtually ceased to exist; their lands lay empty. Certainly the Maori grip on much of New Zealand was enfeebled.

Inland, there was more wealth. New Zealand flax, flourishing in swamps, could be marketed to ropemakers. Yet more valuable was the mighty kauri forest bulking from headland and hill. In terms of timber content the kauri has no peer on the planet; as marine timber it is also unrivalled. From as early as 1800 ships had come seeking the timber of the giant trees Cook reported. Two or three decades on, the quest for kauri had become a stampede. Maori tribesmen provided the labour, trimming and pit-sawing the logs they felled; then the timber was sped to far lands. New Zealand had its first shipyard in 1827, in the Hokianga Harbour, where three kauri vessels were crafted.

The kauri was also used to build the first durable European dwellings, meant to house other, gentler arrivals from the outer world. These were not men in pursuit of earthly riches. They had a tale of mankind's crucified saviour: they talked peace and goodwill rather than profits. The first formal Christian sermon was preached by Sydney's Reverend Samuel Marsden on Christmas Day 1814. He then launched lay missionaries on the land. Winning boisterous Maori souls was, for a decade or two, an uphill enterprise. A musket said more to a warrior than a psalm. Pitiless inter-tribal wars continued; thousands more unconverted Maori perished. There were casualties among the early missionaries too. The most impressive fall was that of Thomas Kendall who, trying to investigate traditional Maori theology, finished up bedding with a Maori woman as a confessed heathen. Others were tempted less by flesh than by land speculation. But by the end of the 1820s Christ's candle was burning brighter in a strange land. Hundreds, then thousands of tribesmen and women — some surely sickened by the unprecedented slaughter of the decade — began calling themselves Christian. Missionary communities rose the length of New Zealand.

More European dwellings did too. From the first, Maori tribes had sought Europeans (*pakeha*) they could call their own. They brought trade, new tools, new foods, and new knowledge. If sold land which lay between fiercely warring tribes, as often happened, they could serve to muffle and dampen menace. Otherwise New Zealand was a no man's land, a beachcomber's Eden; no European power had claimed it. But now long-staying guests were heaving their sea-kits ashore, buying up Maori acres, building homes, and beginning to farm. Something had to happen, and did.

In the early 1830s Britain established a resident in the Bay of Islands. No longer terra incognita, New Zealand was at first seen as an unmanageable appendage of New South Wales. But in Britain there was a scapegrace visionary who saw more powerful potential in the country. More than any man then alive, he would determine the fate of New Zealand. Edward Gibbon Wakefield was to build a career on a country he had never seen. Serving a sentence in Newgate prison for attempting to abscond with an heiress, he grew appalled at the human wastage of his newly industrial land, and wanted New Zealand to be settled as a better Britain. The American experience need not be repeated; nor need notions of human equality be permitted to poison a colony's soul. The price of land, if set sufficiently high, would keep democracy at bay and yeomen in their place. Land? Whose land? The Maori race figured in his scheme of things only as sellers of soil. There was no role for them thereafter. Nevertheless Wakefield won wealthy backers and founded the New Zealand Company. In 1839 land was hastily purchased from Maori for settlements at Wellington, Taranaki, and Nelson: and in 1840 the first colonists were landing in Wellington.

Reluctant to the last, Britain began burdening itself with a new and possibly troublesome colony. Its hand was forced from another quarter. Missionaries and humanitarians wished New Zealand colonised to protect its native people from corruption and land-hungry predators. Then there was France. For 70 years French explorers had been as active as British in mapping New Zealand and defining its nature. There were Frenchmen who saw virtue in New Zealand as a Gallic colony. In the south, land had already been bought.

A relatively humble naval officer, Captain James Hobson, was dispatched from Sydney to annex and govern New Zealand. Missionaries, for the most part, were his advisers in this daunting assignment. The result was a resonant document called the Treaty of Waitangi. It guaranteed Maori rights to traditional lands and fisheries in return for surrender of sovereignty to Queen Victoria. At Waitangi on 6 February 1840, after loud debate, tribal chiefs began appending their names — more often their marks — to the document. Some abstained. Many plainly had little or no notion of what sovereignty meant. The Maori and English texts differed significantly in usage of the word. On the other hand it *was* a remarkable document, given the character of the age, one in which most Europeans thought they had a God-given right to rule without questions asked. For the first time in the history of European colonisation, a native people had been approached as equal partners. The letter of the Treaty has been breached many times in the century and a half since it was signed; its spirit persists. When Maori seek to remedy past injustice, to reclaim lands and fisheries lost through fraud or war, they quote the Treaty of Waitangi chapter and verse to kindle the conscience of their fellow New Zealanders; and with more and more success.

After 1840, the European population grew steadily; it would soon outnumber native Maori. Founded on an isthmus depopulated by the musket, under volcanic cones fashioned into fortresses by its earlier inhabitants, Auckland first functioned as the colony's capital. The New Zealand Company settlements of Wellington, Nelson and New Plymouth were followed by others at Napier, Wanganui, Christchurch and Dunedin.

War and gold made the 1860s New Zealand's most dramatic decade. In the south migrants had spread across the land with ease, with sheepmen pushing their flocks higher and higher into the Southern Alps. Reduced and dispirited by disease and tribal war, southern Maori parted with their land cheaply. In the South Island's one clash over land, 22 colonists were left dead; and British authorities judged the Maori response reasonable. Not a metre of the island was to be taken by conquest.

The North Island's was a sadder story. Tribes were still large and powerful. They were also reluctant to sell, and for good reason. Under missionary tutelage they made huge agricultural advances. They not only fed European settlements; they exported their produce to Australia and California in their own vessels. Landless colonists, penned up in Auckland, looked on with envy.

Maori self-sufficiency also made for a new Maori identity. Central North Island tribes, the most menaced by European land hunger, crowned a Maori King to check the authority of Queen Victoria; they set themselves against further land sales. British sovereignty was put to the test. A war over disputed land sales reddened Taranaki first. A gunboat-backed invasion of the Waikato followed. In the 1860s the British fielded up to 18,000 troops, many of them regulars and veterans of the Crimea, against 1200 occasional warriors at most. Heady Maori triumphs or near-triumphs in such engagements as Rangiriri and Gate Pa proved brief and illusory. Britain's regiments, as fiercely tribal as Maori war parties, finally rolled ruthlessly over opposition; patriotism was no match for disciplined firepower. Set piece battles soon gave way to muddy and murderous campaigns in the jungle-like vegetation of the North Island interior, with armed prophets like Poverty Bay's Te Kooti and Taranaki's Titokowaru trying and failing to rally their race from forest strongholds. The flash and thunder of the twelve-year conflict, however, tends to fog the fact that most Maori circumspectly stood aside from armed rebellion, either taking a neutral position or siding energetically with Britain.

The South Island was alight with another drama, one which would also determine New Zealand's future. Gold was discovered in arid and mountainous Otago in 1861. Tens of thousands of goldseekers were soon storming alpine citadels, surviving blizzards, and wresting fat nuggets from the stormy rivers. Then wet and forested Westland, on the other side of the alps, proved as lucrative. The North Island wasn't altogether left out. The quartz of the Coromandel Peninsula was enriching too, though there craft and capital were needed to get at the gold. In Otago and Westland, New Zealand produced the last of the Pacific's great alluvial rushes, human surges which drew veteran diggers from California and Victoria, and hopeful men and women from all over the globe. Thereafter there were no goldfields left to conquer. Many stayed and used modest windfalls to farm or go into business or trade. Canny and Scottish Dunedin had made the most of the bonanza at its back door and became New Zealand's first significant city and a source of capital to revive the war-wearied north.

One way and another New Zealand's population grew spectacularly. An even more lasting legacy was the egalitarianism of the goldfields; it would colour New Zealand's character and find expression in political form before the nineteenth century was out. This wasn't how Edward Gibbon Wakefield had foreseen it; but he was already in the grave, a disappointed colonial politician and failed midwife to a new Britain. Nevertheless New Zealand, as we now recognise it, was born.

Earth's bounty built New Zealand.

Built New Zealanders too.

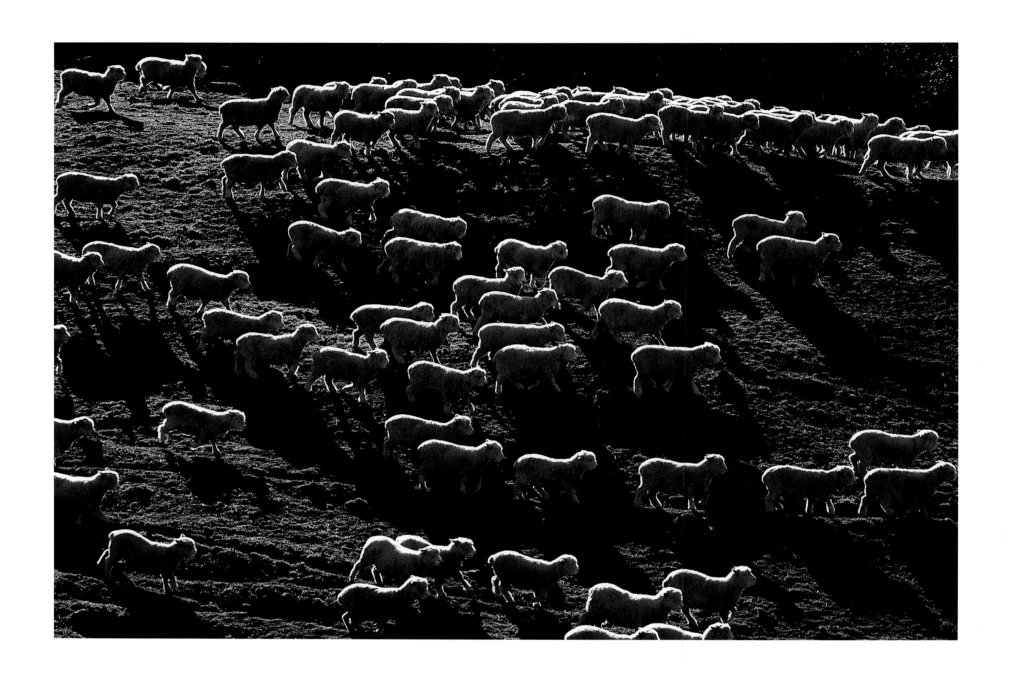

Some countrymen graze.

Others grow.

Always close to the earth,
the countryman stands with
an eye to the world's weather.

Their flocks carpet high ground.

Their crops colour low.

The sea holds
another harvest.

And has since Polynesians
first cast nets in these islands.

Man-made forest now bestrides desert and dune.

Tribesmen who once felled trees but for canoes now crop wood for the world.

Industry grows too.

Where once was rural calm,
industrial fires roar.

Energy is the name of the new game.
The native energy of these islands.

Old needs, new ways.

Ways to wealth in this land.

Man's work rivals nature's.

The human forest is here.

Some cities sit shy on a stark shore.

Elsewhere they march bold.

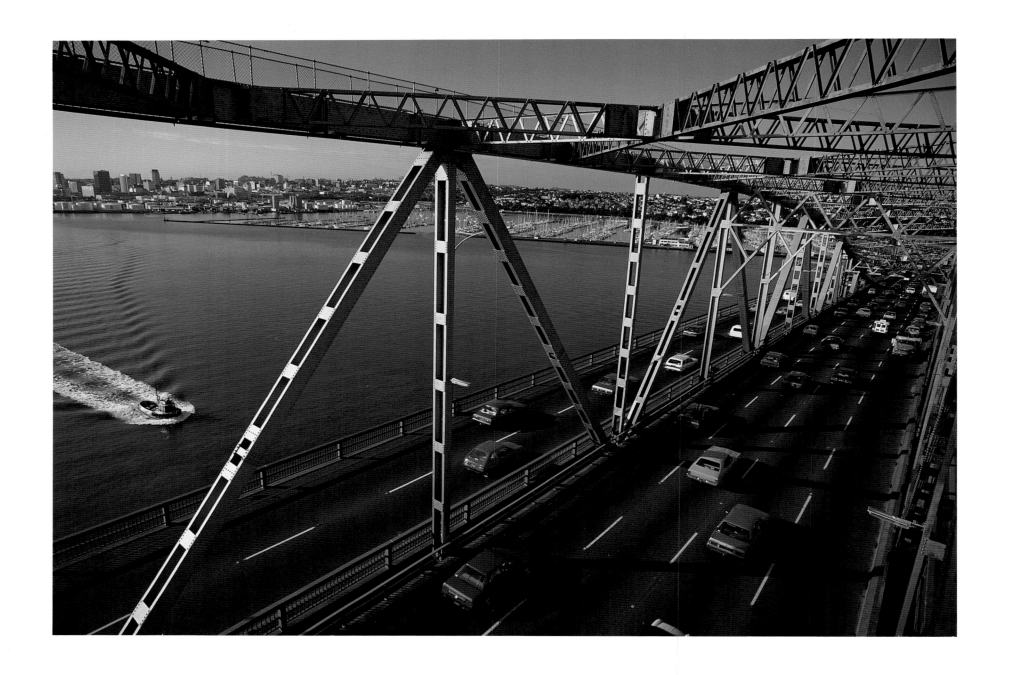

All built to do business with the world.

Often with grace.

Always with power.

*Most New Zealanders now
know the city as home.*

More and more, the cities are
a mix of face and race.

Europe, Polynesia and Asia
meet in the marketplace.

Some suburbs sprawl.

Some climb.

Others crawl.

Some into mists where older, leafy New Zealand still lives.

By the end of the nineteenth century New Zealand was drawing less and less on the easy riches of the land. The whale herds had long gone, the seals too. The great kauri forests had largely been felled. The country's gold resided in distant bank vaults. The people of this new South Pacific society were left with one large resource to draw on. That resource was the land.

One innovation of the 1880s — refrigeration — was to confirm the country's fate. After the frozen meat trade began, the colony was unmistakably a bread basket for Britain: a basket brimming with butter, cheese, and fat lamb. The wool of the land's flocks kept the wheels of Britain's textile mills turning. It has been said, with some truth, that the story of New Zealand agriculture is the story of New Zealand. Nowhere is this more apparent than in the last two decades of the nineteenth century. The South Island, often open tussock country with large flocks grazing, was fast to prosper from the new boost to pastoral farming. In the North Island forests began blazing, summer after summer, as hundreds of thousands of hectares were claimed for sheep and cattle. The farmer, soon typically seen as a brawny smallholder in gumboots and black singlet, was hailed as the backbone of the country; his voice in the country's legislative chambers would become powerful. In the 1890s many large estates were broken up to give such small farmers a fatter share of the colonial pie.

It wasn't all a hay-ride. Pioneer hardships were many; soul-crushing isolation, loneliness and backbreak were the rule, particularly in remote and still roadless pockets of the North Island where men scattered grass seed in the ashes of incinerated forest, with skeletal trees rising stark around. Yet even the most brutal landscape was coloured with human optimism; migrant Britons found a freedom here unknown in their birthplace. This was the land of milk and honey, colonial boosters said: this was a workingman's paradise. Some found a Biblical promise fulfilled: 'The Lord thy God bringeth thee into a good land, a land of brooks and water, of fountains and depths that spring out of valleys and hills . . . a land of oil, olive and honey; a land where thou shalt eat bread without scarceness . . .

Politicians did nothing to discourage such fervour. 'God's Own Country,' boomed Richard John Seddon, New Zealand's burly turn-of-century premier. The notion became conventional wisdom, even on the other side of the world. In Britain the *Labourers Union Chronicle* urged its readers to 'rush from the old doomed country to such a paradise as New Zealand'. Belief in an antipodean Eden wasn't built altogether on blind faith. For the newcomers, fled from skies darkened by industrialism, there *was* a clean world of sufficiency and

157

independence oceans away from Europe's extremes of want and wealth. It has been persuasively argued that late nineteenth century New Zealand did, in great part, measure up to the Arcadian vision, perhaps more so than any society in history. It wasn't to last, but it was good while it did. The tales told by our grandparents may once have seemed sentimental and wishful; they more and more look to have been true.

The long-lived Liberal administration of ex-goldfield storekeeper Seddon led New Zealand into the twentieth century. It also, according to many onlookers, led the world. State intervention had been seen as necessary to cure the chronic economic ills of the colony, to undertake large capital works; and above all to relieve the afflictions of urban and rural poor. Female suffrage — with New Zealand again leading the world — was soon taken for granted; so also were pensions for the old and impoverished. It wasn't an experiment born of socialist ideologists. It was essentially the response of enlightened and pragmatic politicians to human need. An American scholar saw New Zealand as 'the social laboratory of the world', a phrase which was to reverberate long into the century. Conservatives saw the founding of the world's first welfare state as recklessly Utopian. Radicals, such as a still obscure Russian named Lenin, saw New Zealand's example as an attempt to buy off revolution with reform. Whatever it was, the belief that the State knew best, and did best, was to serve New Zealanders well into the new century. After 1900 most New Zealanders were native born, and a new generation of politicians reflected the fact. Spiritually as well as physically they seemed a world away from the land their parents left.

Yet New Zealand remained part of the world, and especially part of the British Empire. A near mystical belief in the benevolence of the Empire, and the virtue of the British crown, held native nationalism in check. New Zealanders lacked a useful notion of themselves and looked to the Empire for identity. Young New Zealanders were educated as little Britons; they knew Britain's history, not their own. Interest in what New Zealand was, and might be, was confined to romantics and a few wistful writers, not least Thomas Bracken, whose memorial was to be our now national song, 'God Defend New Zealand', with its impeccably democratic sentiments. But nationalist noises were faint beside the Empire's drum. Beating it was a routinely vote-winning exercise for politicians, more so as Europe rumbled with rumours of war. New Zealand contributed a dreadnought to Britain's navy. It introduced conscription long before Britain thought to. It applauded British generals who arrived to warn of conflict to come.

In 1914 the Empire at last had business for New Zealand; that business was killing. Britain declared war on Germany on New Zealand's behalf. Not only did the country have no choice in the matter: if the cheering crowds in the streets were to be believed, or the queues outside recruiting offices counted, it didn't want one. New Zealand troops raced to capture Western Samoa, the first German territory to be taken in World War I; the only loss was perspiration.

But there was lethal business ahead. An expeditionary force of 10,000 young New Zealanders joined with 20,000 Australians on the way to the trenches of France. This antipodean army — soon to be called the Australian and New Zealand Army Corps, or 'Anzacs' — had its journey cut short at Suez. The British high command had another use for them; they were to play a part in a seaborne assault on Turkey, to strike and seize the Gallipoli peninsula above the slender sea-lane known as the Dardanelles. It was one of the most inept excursions in the history of armed conflict, poorly planned and led by posturing fantasists. In six months of horror no more than a few hundred worthless hectares of Turkey were taken. At the end, nearly 3000 New Zealanders were left on Turkey's heights; more were carried off maimed in mind and body. The price of pride in the British Empire was high.

All the same, New Zealand won some identity for itself in the agony of that offensive. Another 15,000 New Zealanders were to fall fighting for Mother Britain in World War I, proportionately the greatest combatant loss suffered by any country involved; but the lives wasted by elegantly blundering British leaders in the short-lived Gallipoli campaign were the most angrily recalled. For the first time New Zealanders were aware that they were, after all, not Britons; that they were distinct even from the Australians they often fought alongside. But who were they? National feeling born of battle had next to no cultural tradition to feed on. European New Zealand had precious little literature, art, music and theatre it could call its own; its popular culture was for the most part imported; its folklore was still forming. That which had deep roots in the land was mostly borrowed from the Maori. Back home nationalism seldom rose louder than bitter whispers at regimental reunions. The euphoria of the war's end left notions of independence high and dry. Officially New Zealand was still the most loyal land in the British Empire. It seemed set to prove itself so again in 1939, on the outbreak of World War II. New Zealand's then Labour prime minister, Michael Joseph Savage, announced that where Britain stood, we stood. It is not a declaration a politician would risk now.

Ironically Savage's government had until then taken a cautiously independent stance in international affairs. It had also led New Zealand out of world depression, with large public works and housing programmes, and had reinforced and expanded the welfare state in defiance of prevailing economic wisdom. The Depression had demonstrated how vulnerable New Zealand was to the cold winds of the world. A drive for greater self-sufficiency saw the State backing native industries, and imposing stiff import duties on outside competitors. Such a policy not only produced jobs, but also did much to ensure the country's economic independence. For a time it seemed New Zealand had seen a sea-change. But when the crunch came, and war, pious imperial sentiments still served politicians best.

New Zealand troops, early in the theatre of war, were bundled into campaigns — in Greece, and then Crete — almost as desperate and disastrous as that on Gallipoli; nothing had been learned. But thereafter New Zealand politicians took a larger and more critical interest in what the British high command did with their troops. Nerve failed them, though, when Japan entered the war and swept down the Pacific. Australia called its troops back to defend its own shores. New Zealand did not: New Zealand troops continued battling from North Africa up into Italy. Back home on leave, though, many veterans rebelled, refusing to return to Europe. They had read the message, even if their leaders had not. New Zealand's business was in the Pacific, not in Europe.

That has become even more plain in the decades since the war. The end of Empire, followed by Britain's economic marriage to continental Europe, was to loosen old imperial links. New Zealand has settled for not especially onerous membership of the British Commonwealth of Nations, with a British monarch, represented by native-born Governors-General as nominal heads of state. A new and more independent breed of New Zealanders has begun to make itself heard, culturally, socially and politically. Historians like Keith Sinclair and poets like Allen Curnow have helped their fellow countrymen make sense of their past and given them a more profound feeling for the present. New Zealand's native accent is more and more apparent, and not least in art, crafts and letters. In the 1930s Curnow's vivid lines looked forward from post-colonial dependence to national independence:

'Not I, some child born in a marvellous year,
Will learn the trick of standing upright here.'

In the 1980s New Zealanders were learning to stand upright with no difficulty, and more and more pride. Their country was to risk the rancour of Britain, the United States and even its erstwhile Anzac partner Australia, in declaring itself non-nuclear. Support for such a stand cut across conventional political lines. It seemed the message of Gallipoli had at last been heard: New Zealand was not to be a plaything of great powers again.

The limitations of a solo stance, however, were demonstrated in 1985, when French terrorists shamelessly sank the anti-nuclear protest vessel *Rainbow Warrior* on the Auckland waterfront, killing a crewman. An aggrieved New Zealand looked to the United States and Britain for sympathy and support, and found neither. Finally French economic blackmail persuaded New Zealand, in effect, to surrender the two terrorists imprisoned. New Zealand was suddenly an orphan in an unruly world. The national climate was new; it was also bracing.

Other things changed too. A new Labour government appeared to reject the work of its predecessors, slashing away regulations and controls which had encrusted the economy for forty years. State intervention, of the kind which had long distinguished New Zealand, had no place in the new scheme of things. Subsidies and incentives were ended, import restrictions too. The outside world arrived with a rush. State-owned enterprises were sold off. Agriculture and industry alike had to stand on their own feet. The results were painful, with farmers leaving their land and job queues lengthening. The promise was that in the fullness of time stern measures would be gainful. For better or worse there is one thing to be said. New Zealand is now itself, making its own history, not living that of others. No one could deny New Zealand nationhood now.

FACES OF THE NATION

This is a land of more than three million faces.

Each with its own story. Here let them speak.

It remains a land of more cultures than one,
of craftsman and artist.

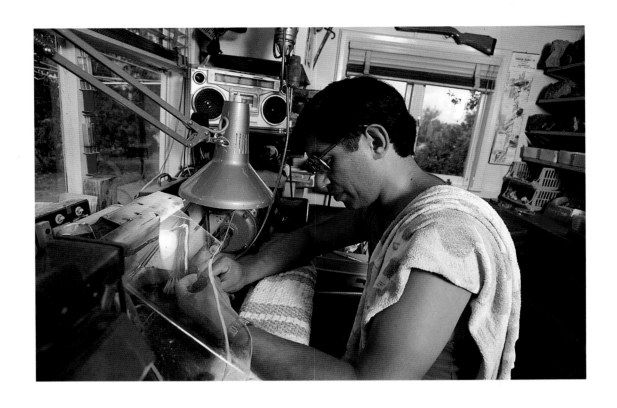

Tomorrow's New Zealand? What are we?
Who? The nation is still in the making.

Rugby's oval ball unites the nation.

Many test themselves against wind and tide.

Or current and river.

For others, hoofbeats may be more to the point.

Or hunting old-world style.

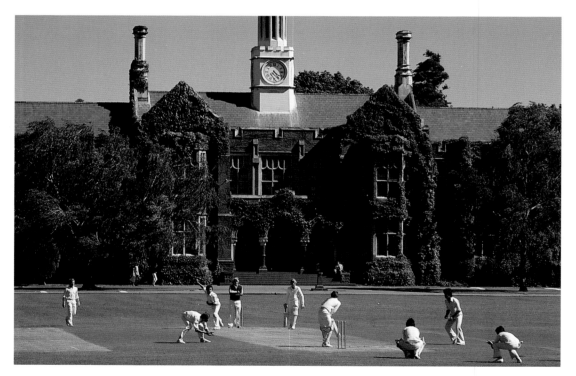

Games from old homelands.

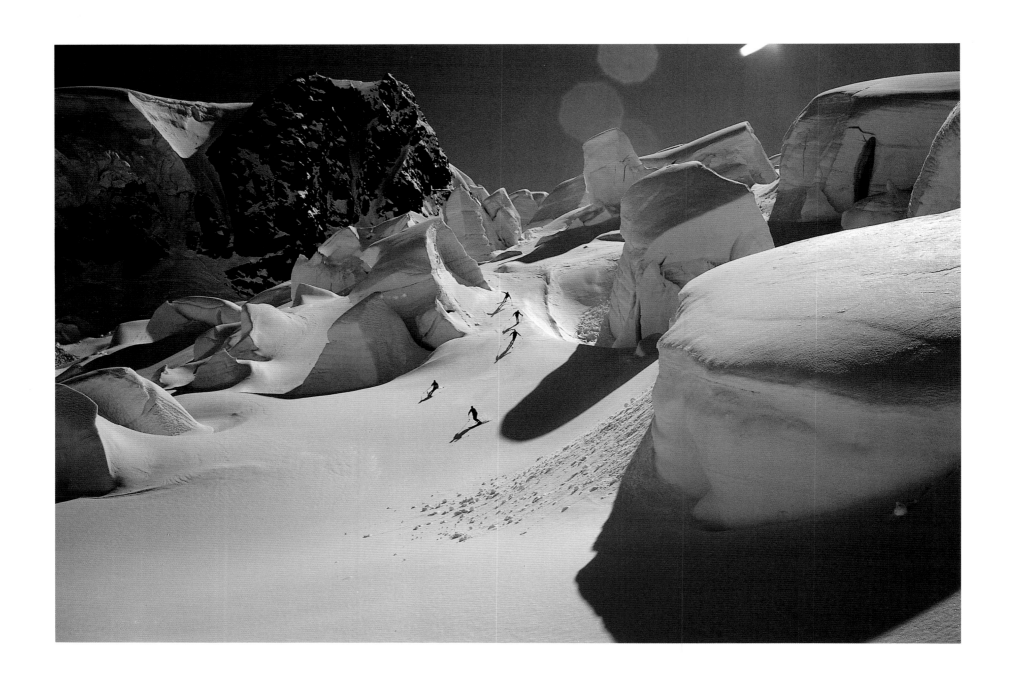

Sports of a new.

The fish of the rivers
are there for the winning,
the fruits of the sea.

And the tides of the seasons.
Loneliness in an uncrowded land is a loved pursuit.

Distance has long determined New Zealand's nature — distance from great continents, great cities, great marketplaces and cultures. When Polynesians colonised the country, they lost all link with the tropical islands from which they had sailed. They faintly recalled a spiritual homeland called Hawaiki, a name to be found on no map, and believed their souls soared back there after the death of the body. The belief intriguingly suggests that New Zealand — or Aotearoa, as they named their discovery — was still considered too new, no fit place for life everlasting. But their theology did change to accommodate their solitary situation. Polynesia's gods and heroes took on new roles, and new names; there were new legends to live by. Distance, and oceanic isolation, fertilised the flowering of one of the Pacific's most spirited cultures.

For Europeans, arriving 800 years later, distance was measurable in miles or kilometres. New Zealand is 8000 kilometres from Asia, 7000 from South America, 19,000 from Europe. Even Australia is most of 2000 daunting kilometres away. Small wonder that the next arrivals sometimes also had a wistful and faraway gaze. Their Hawaiki mostly lay in the North Sea; for Asian migrants on the goldfields it was somewhere in south China where their bodies would one day be shipped for burial. Pale-skinned colonists may not have believed that their spirits fled back to Britain, or arranged for their bodies to be returned to native soil. There was no need. In spirit many still dwelled there more than a century after their great-grandfathers arrived on migrant vessels. British novelist Anthony Trollope had already summed the country up in the 1870s: 'The New Zealander among John Bulls is the most John Bullish . . . he is more English than the Englishman at home.'

'Home', until two or three decades ago, was the common New Zealand name for Britain. Long after political independence had been won, New Zealand remained a spiritual appendage of Britain. In the 1940s, after World War II, New Zealand — as a patriotic gesture — sold its produce to Britain below ruling prices. As late as 1951, the worst epithet a politician could use to damn striking trade unionists was to call them un-British.

Nations are made of more than trade and politics. There is sport, for example. Ironically it was a game devised by and for English public schoolboys which was to unify the country as nothing else has. The oval-ball game began in New Zealand a century ago. From early in the twentieth century, brawny and speedy New Zealand rugby teams were humbling the best other nations could field; New Zealanders roared their approval as one. It was a warrior game, underlined

195

by the *haka*, the Maori war-dance, which New Zealand teams use to please crowds and intimidate opponents before an international encounter.

There was another, subtler and finally more durable subterranean growth of nationalist temper in the early decades of the twentieth century, though it was not to be evident until much more of the century had passed. That growth was in the arts. New Zealanders had at last begun singing their own songs.

Until mid-century the representative New Zealand artists were short-story writer Katherine Mansfield and painter Frances Hodgkins. They had one thing in common. Both were expatriate. Both made their name in Europe before they were embraced by their native land; both felt the lack of a society, a sympathetic audience, to nourish their work here. Yet Hodgkins always craved the good opinion of her fellow New Zealanders. Even in sophisticated Mansfield there was a sturdy nationalist streak. 'I want', she wrote, 'to make our undiscovered country leap into the eyes of the Old World.' Which she did, in some of the most luminous stories in the English language. She never returned to New Zealand other than in the imagination.

Many in succeeding generations were to make the European voyage too. The difference was that they began to voyage home again. Some, in fact, never left. Their home was here, for better and worse, with much of the latter. From the 1930s on, characteristic artists were Frank Sargeson, a short-story writer, holed up in a mean suburban shack to dedicate himself to his craft and the sound of the New Zealand voice; and the painter Eric Lee-Johnson, leading a nomadic and impoverished existence in one small community after another while he laboured to persuade New Zealanders to look at their land with more love. Both had made the European journey and returned; both remained unsung and unknown to most of their compatriots; both, in showing New Zealand raw, gave offence to the existing and enfeebled status quo in the arts — a tradition of genteel Georgian verse and refined watercolours.

A generation later, though, the picture was dramatically different. It is most robustly illustrated in the life of Colin McCahon, the most potent and most truly native New Zealand painter of this century. Not for McCahon a European journey. The see-sawing battle of light and dark over the hills and mountains of the South Island was a larger inspiration than any Europe's galleries could offer. 'I saw', he said, 'something logical, orderly and beautiful belonging to the land and not yet to its people. Not yet understood or communicated, not even yet really invented.'

There is an echo of Mansfield's passionate declaration here. The difference is that McCahon was not interested in making New Zealand 'leap into the eyes of the Old World' — he wanted New Zealand, logical, orderly and beautiful, to leap into the eyes of its own people. Understanding and communicating New Zealand became his lifetime mission. For a while that mission met silence at best, mockery at worst. But by the time of his death, in 1987, his heroic stature was plain. His vision of the land had become common coin. He died in a decade when the arts had at last begun to wrest some of the nation's high ground from sporting heroes and heroines. New Zealand poets, painters, composers, playwrights, sculptors and craftsmen were all taken for granted. New Zealanders understood their country and themselves better.

A New Zealand writer to match McCahon in vision was the poet James K. Baxter. The son of a savagely maltreated World War I conscientious objector, and seldom to forget it, his relationship with his land was always boisterous and bittersweet. 'These unshaped islands, on the sawyer's bench,' he wrote, 'Wait for the chisel of the mind.' It might have been Mansfield again, or McCahon. All three were haunted by the heady notion of making the land live in their art. Baxter goes on to talk of 'the swampy towns/Like dreamers struggling to wake/Longing for the poet's truth/And the lover's pride'.

He was to give his country more of a poet's truth than it was ready to accept. There was a lover's pride in his birthplace too, and especially in his pioneering Scots forebears, 'those Gaelic-speaking men and women, descending with their bullock trains and baggage to cross the mouth of the Brighton river . . . the earth lay before them, for that one moment of history, as a primitive and sacred bride'.

Before his short life ended, he turned to the Maori for that tribal feeling of his ancestors; and especially for the spirit of *aroha* (love, and goodwill) which permeates tribal gatherings. He took a Maori Christian name, Hemi, and was lamented and buried as a tribesman. New Zealand letters has a story no stranger.

A quest as heroic as McCahon's, as haunting as Baxter's, was that of the Maori carver Pine Taiapa. Traditional Maori arts and crafts had all but perished by the twentieth century, and as part of a programme for racial survival, a school for Maori arts was founded at Rotorua. As a young pupil, Pine was bitter when he found an establishment producing no more than cheap curios for tourists. His teachers could copy, not create; imagination and craft had gone with most of the tales and traditions of the race. Yet Pine knew those tales and traditions; his rich and wild work, drawing on mythology, baffled his supposed masters. In months he was teaching his teachers; in a year he had charge of the school.

There was one large lack. With chisel, mallet and gouge alone — which was what carvers were reduced to by the 1920s — there was no way of winning the sweep and flow of the old masterpieces of Maori carving. How to emulate the giants who carved them? Pine dreamed the answer: the adze. The carvers of the past had worked first with the adze, trimming wood down to free and fine shape; the chisel was used only for surface decoration. But who knew the use of the adze now? Might there be one old craftsman, somewhere, who knew?

With that hope Pine travelled for months looking for one old craftsman with a memory. Weary and close to quitting, he heard of an old farmer named Eramiha Kapua in bush country near Te Teko. Though he no longer carved, yes, he knew the adze; he knew the songs to sing to make wood live.

Pine bore his prize back to Rotorua; his school had its first professor. And Maori carving lived again, with new vision and vigour. Work which once took weeks could be done in days. For Pine himself the old tool was revelation and inspiration. A hurricane of a carver, working close to twenty hours a day, this passionate giant with adze and chisel was to leave more than one hundred buildings in his wake, and scores of talented pupils, before he died in 1972. His dream had been to make the art of his race live again, so modern Maori might flourish. He saw that art survive; he saw his faltering race rise again.

A nation is people, and New Zealand grows more diverse by the decade. If there is a typical New Zealand face it is no longer quite white, no longer quite brown. The movement of native Maori from old tribal lands to the cities gathered pace after World War II; racial intermarriage became even more commonplace. Officially the Maori race now numbers over 400,000, most of mixed blood. Unofficially scores of thousands of other New Zealanders claim Maori ancestry. Maori were followed by migrants from tropical Polynesia, from Tonga, Samoa, and the Cook and Tokelau Islands. They now number more than the Maori did in mid-century, and possibly as many as another 200,000; many were born here and know no other homeland. Now an Asian influx, heralded by Vietnamese refugees, and the largest since the goldrushes of the last century, has begun. New Zealand cities have shed their dour colonial colour. There is plainly a new, distinctive and humanly richer society in the making. New Zealand, in the words of poet Allen Curnow, has always been 'something nobody counted on'.

Distance is of the past; the isolation that determined much of New Zealand's story too. The arrival of air travel means Europe is a day away, and North America less. Television means instant images of the world outside. New Zealanders are citizens of that world, stirred by the same hopes and fears as their fellows. As planetary survival becomes an issue they at last seem in the same boat as the rest of the human race, more and more willing to take the oars, no longer a comfortable, complacent and half-forgotten people at the foot of the globe.

The character of the larger cities still partakes of the past. Spreading and sprawling Auckland remains as it began, haphazard and unplanned. Its glassy centre is brash and commercial, rich in boom and bust, its suburbs more and more divided socially. Conscious of its responsibilities as capital, Wellington has a stiffer, more democratic character, something born of its boisterous situation beside the Cook Strait, where wind and storm make all men kin, but perhaps too of the rebellious New Zealand Company migrants who struck for their rights, and won the eight-hour day, soon after they were set down on a stark shore. Rich in nineteenth century Gothic architecture, Christchurch cannot help but make a feast of its pilgrim beginnings; Olde England on an antipodean shore has become a moneyspinner for the tourist trade. Dunedin, by contrast, doesn't have to try. New Zealand's once largest community, born of the goldrush, has become one of the world's most elegant Victorian cities. Developers have largely left it alone; it has the quality of a place with three or four centuries of settled existence. The anguish which once attended the flow of capital and population to the north has largely passed. The unlovely glass towers and brutal traffic of Auckland have begun telling Dunedin's citizens that they are, after all, on to a good thing.

In the end, as at the beginning, there is the land. Man may have refashioned or befouled it: its arresting and often awesome character has never been killed. In the twentieth century, not before time, governments began locking wilderness into some of the planet's most spectacular national parks. In such places New Zealand's origins are plain wherever the eye rests — a land tossed from the sea floor by terrestrial commotion, modelled by ice and fire, bitten by wind and wave. No sea gave voyaging man a greener gift.

THE LASTING LAND

After a thousand years man's mark remains puny on the land's powerful flanks.
The land was there before he took it as wife. It will surely outlive him as widow.
Maori proverb says all human riches pass; the riches of the land are forever.
Let the ebb and flow of light on the native forms
of New Zealand have the last word.

A new Pacific people, a fresh-minted nation of islanders,
are heir to the contours of a country and a society still in the shaping . . .
Tomorrow's New Zealand may not always be as they want it;
it will surely be as they make it.

Photographic Identification